Montana

TRAVEL JOURNAL

Capture the Memorable Moments
of Your Montana Adventure.

Katie Clemons
Award winning storycatcher
at Gadanke.com

To my dad,
who taught me that when in doubt, the best
place to be is the mountains of Montana.

Gadanke

PO Box 812

Livingston, MT

59047 USA

Design and text by Katie Clemons.

Copyright ©2015 Katie Clemons.

Published in the United States by Katie Clemons LLC.

https://gadanke.com

Printed in USA

ISBN: 978-1-63336-023-5

HITTING THE ROAD

Name:

Age:

Where I'm going:

Who's coming with me:

When we're heading to Montana:

How we're getting there:

What we're packing:

What we're doing:

What we're eager to see:

What we're hoping to try:

When we're going back home:

MONTANA: CAPTURE YOUR ADVENTURE

FOR SEVERAL GENERATIONS, there has been a distinct line drawn into the Montana psyche, separating weekends from the workweek. My family labors Monday through Friday in anticipation of the weekend, when we pull out fishing rods, skis, sleeping bags, shovels, and most likely, our winter coats. There are few months of the year where a winter coat isn't a necessity around this neck of the woods. And I could probably count on my fingers the number of days when air conditioning was requisite.

"The mountains are our air conditioning," my dad always said on the hottest of summer days, packing us into his mud-crusted green Subaru to wander into the cooler Montana mountains.

Outhouses, campfires, and blueberry pancakes were all part of my childhood landscape, as they have been in some form since my family immigrated to Montana Territory in the 1800s. My dad taught my siblings and me to navigate the Montana backcountry, and in turn, our lives. I learned the arts of patience and silence as we watched grazing elk or dipped our hooked worms into the flowing creeks where the water ran so clear that trout could look right up and see us peering down.

I'm trying to teach my toddler son that silence now. "Niklas!" I shout-whisper. "Come see it." He drops whatever book he's reading or blocks he's stacking and rushes to my side. He scrambles up the step stool and onto the cedar chest of heirloom pillowcases and linens. He scans the horizon, and then I know he's got those deer in sight.

"See it! See it! See it!" he squeals wildly.

The deer throw their heads into the air on full alert. Their ears stand straight and they do not move.

Meanwhile, Niklas is doing a happy dance that involves every inch of his less-than-three-foot body. He continues squealing and prepares to start banging on the windows like he is a caged monkey in the zoo and the deer have come to watch.

I imagine them bedding down on the other hillside at night, chatting about their day and that silly boy they saw in that house.

What Niklas doesn't know is that my dad and I both get as excited as he does when we spot deer. It's only age and knowing the virtue of silence that keeps us relatively calm. Our telephone conversations usually begin, "Have the deer been out there? Has Niklas seen them?"

There's something addictive about this place. Montana resonates deep in your heart, wherever you go, like the mud caked in layers on that old Subaru. I think you'll feel it too, as you explore.

Thank you for purchasing this journal, one of the many volumes I've written to help folks like you celebrate your story, document your life, and find greater joy and gratitude with your whole heart. For more journaling guidance and storycatching inspiration, come visit me at Gadanke.com. Share your story at #mygadankejournal. I'd love to see how you're using your journal and where you're traveling in Montana!

TWO WAYS TO SEE: WIDTH AND DEPTH

Become a storycatcher by gathering your experiences and tucking them into the pockets of your journal. One way to do this is by viewing your vacation in two ways, broadly and closely—or as I say, width and depth.

Observe the big picture of your trip by paying attention to what's around you: herds of animals, thousands of trees, mountains, folks of various sorts doing their thing, etc. These observations set the scene of your stories. They establish your sense of place, and they're fun to sketch. Scenic postcards help capture these moments as well.

Also look deeply and hone into some of your experiences. Examine details like the smell of pine and wildflowers on your walk or the taste of huckleberry pie. Record bits of conversation with a stranger. Add memorabilia like ticket stubs, receipts, or pressed flowers to your journal. Looking deeply is seeing and watching one bison more than the herd. These observations are what make your journal rich, because they don't just narrate what's around you. They tell your story and answer questions like why and how.

The writing prompts on the following pages remind you to share both the width and depth of your story so you can easily recall your experiences. Life continues on, but the handwritten details of these moments will keep the memories fresh.

HERE'S HOW YOUR JOURNAL WORKS

From pages 24 to 37, you will find what I call Daily Entry pages with writing prompts that begin "Details that make today sensational" and "Brief summary of today." Use these pages to jot down quick five-minute notes about the events that happen each day. This sequential record is perfect for jogging your memory when you have more time to expand your stories.

The rest of the writing prompts are yours to have fun with. Pass them around and invite other people to add their stories. Try sketching. Do some leaf rubbings. Make lists. Press flowers. Write paragraphs. Tuck in mementos, photos, and brochures with double-sided tape or scrapbook adhesive. Your Montana adventures will take on a whole new dimension just by pausing to capture them in this journal.

It's your story. Don't stress out about it being the perfect story. Just focus on what you see and experience. Celebrate what makes you feel alive—that's what you want to record.

Me? I cross out words in my journal all the time. I skip pages. I tear out parts or leave things blank. To avoid something I call "blank page syndrome," sometimes I don't even start on page one! There are no rules. Go easy on yourself. Enjoy the journey. Or as we say in my hometown of Butte, Montana: "Tap 'er light!"

I'll see you out there. We'll try to be quiet. Don't want to spook those deer!

♡ Katie

THE ITINERARY

Adventure begins:

JAN	JUL	1	2	3	4	5	6	7
FEB	AUG	8	9	10	11	12	13	14
MAR	SEP	15	16	17	18	19	20	21
APR	OCT							
MAY	NOV	22	23	24	25	26	27	28
JUN	DEC	29	24	31				

Trip notes:

Adventure wraps up:

JAN	JUL	1	2	3	4	5	6	7
FEB	AUG	8	9	10	11	12	13	14
MAR	SEP	15	16	17	18	19	20	21
APR	OCT							
MAY	NOV	22	23	24	25	26	27	28
JUN	DEC	29	24	31				

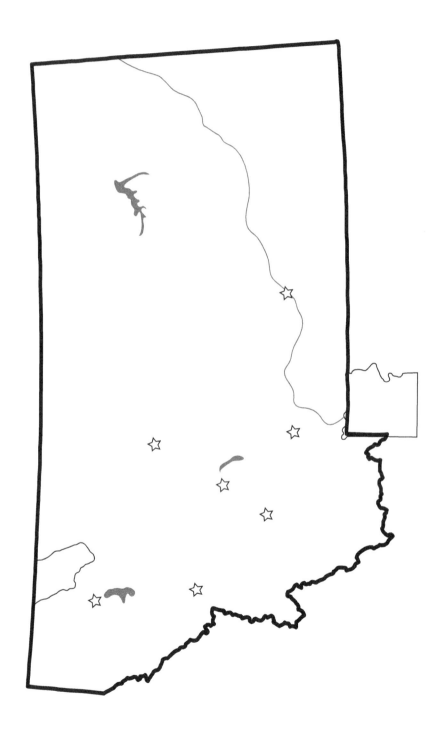

Our route:

DAILY ENTRY PAGES

EACH DAY, TRY TO spend a few minutes filling out one of the following pages. It's easy, just read the prompt and jot down what comes to mind.

With so many new experiences, it is sometimes difficult to remember exactly what you saw and experienced each day. Did you see that bear yesterday on the way out of Glacier National Park? Or was it in the park the day before? And what was the name of that town with the old-fashioned, handmade candy shop. Philipsburg? Petersburg? Oh dear.

Our minds can blur the details . . . unless we write them down! Creating a daily documenting routine provides a reservoir of information for a later time when you want to dive deep into storytelling.

So write away, and try to do it every day. These pages are your little gold nuggets from the foothills to mine one by one.

DETAILS THAT MAKE
today sensational

Today looked like:

Today smelled like:

Today tasted like:

Today sounded like:

Today felt like:

DATE: _____

Brief summary of today

_____

1.

2.

3.

4.

5.

DATE: _____

DETAILS THAT MAKE
today sensational

Today looked like:

Today smelled like:

Today tasted like:

Today sounded like:

Today felt like:

DATE: _____

Brief summary of today

———————————

1.

2.

3.

4.

5.

DATE: _____

DETAILS THAT MAKE
today sensational

Today looked like:

Today smelled like:

Today tasted like:

Today sounded like:

Today felt like:

DATE: _____

Brief summary of today

_____

1.

2.

3.

4.

5.

DATE: _____

DETAILS THAT MAKE
today sensational

Today looked like:

Today smelled like:

Today tasted like:

Today sounded like:

Today felt like:

DATE: _____

Brief summary of today

———————————

1.

2.

3.

4.

5.

DATE: _____

DETAILS THAT MAKE
today sensational

Today looked like:

Today smelled like:

Today tasted like:

Today sounded like:

Today felt like:

DATE: _____

Brief summary of today

_____

1.

2.

3.

4.

5.

DATE: _____

DETAILS THAT MAKE
today sensational

Today looked like:

Today smelled like:

Today tasted like:

Today sounded like:

Today felt like:

DATE: _____

Brief summary of today

_____

1.

2.

3.

4.

5.

DATE: _____

DETAILS THAT MAKE
today sensational

Today looked like:

Today smelled like:

Today tasted like:

Today sounded like:

Today felt like:

DATE: _____

Brief summary of today

———————————

1.

2.

3.

4.

5.

DATE: _____

Taking this trip because . . .

DATE: _____

ONCE IN A LIFETIME

I'm so glad I get to share it with ...

I explore

I ride

I eat

I drink

DATE: _____

I wander

I sleep

I find

I would do it all over again.

THEY CALL ME
"*The Adventurer!*"

•• What I hear ••

Well you don't see
that *every day.*

_____

DATE: _____

- ◆ Been there
- ◆ Done that
- ◆ Saw *a few animals*

• • What takes my breath • •

The food I eat:

_____

DATE: _____

FOR THE RECORD

I am not lost. I am merely
enjoying the terrific views.

DATE: _____

Some *wonderful* moments of this vacation

———————

DATE: _____

DATE: _____

•• What I smell ••

DATE: _____

• • What I'm trying for the first time • •

Wildlife I see

DATE: _____

DATE: _____

Useful things I packed

———————————

Not so useful things I packed

———————————

Oh wow!

I never would've known.

TO WHOM IT MAY CONCERN:
I've got nothing to do and *all day* to do it!

• • What I feel • •

DATE: _____

•• What I'm inspired by ••

Top moments
I LOVE

_1._

_2._

_3._

4.

5.

6.

DATE: _____

WARNING

Beautiful and relaxing
vacations in The Big
Sky State may result
in difficulty returning
to a regular routine on
Monday.

• • What I can't get enough of • •

Gosh, the folks I meet!

In Montana, fishermen are notorious for stretching the truth about the fish that got away—it keeps getting bigger!

_____

This story is nothing *like that.*

•• What I wear ••

DATE: _____

• • *What I carry* • •

• • *What I taste* • •

Then there is the shopping . . .

DATE: _____

SPOTTED:

Deer

Buffalo

Bald Eagle

Man on horseback

Moose

Squirrel or Chipmunk

Marmot

Bear

DATE: _____

Skunk (seen or smelled!)

Wild animal droppings

Waterfall

Montana state flag

Dirt road

Roadkill

Hawk

Cowboy boots

Belt buckle or plaid

Rodeo

Snow

Hiking trail

Fishing spot

Museum

Pickup truck with a dog

Wildflowers

DATE: _____

• • What I see • •

DATE: _____

• • What I want to remember • •

THE BIGGEST
crack-me-up moment

DATE: _____

DATE: _____

Montana truly is
the last best place

Additional writing prompt journals by Katie Clemons:

Journey, travel journal

Between Mom and Me, mother son journal

My Mom and Me, mother daughter journal

You are Loved, baby journal

She, introspective personal journal

Become, diary for finding your direction

Jump Up, kid's time capsule journal

available at gadanke.com

CPSIA information can be obtained
at www.ICGtesting.com
Printed in the USA
LVHW08s1257240918
591178LV00011B/77/P